Country Diary Wales.
Published in Great Britain in 2023 by Graffeg.

Written by John Gilbey copyright © 2023.
Photography by John Gilbey copyright © 2023.
Designed and produced by Graffeg Limited
copyright © 2023.

Graffeg Limited, 24 Stradey Park Business
Centre, Mwrwg Road, Llangennech, Llanelli,
Carmarthenshire, SA14 8YP, Wales, UK.
www.graffeg.com.

John Gilbey is hereby identified as the author of this
work in accordance with section 77 of the Copyright,
Designs and Patents Act 1988.

A CIP Catalogue record for this book is available
from the British Library.

The publisher gratefully acknowledges the financial
support of this book by the Books Council of Wales.
www.gwales.com.

ISBN 9781802581997

Printed in China

1 2 3 4 5 6 7 8 9

MIX
Paper from
responsible sources
FSC® C016973
FSC
www.fsc.org

50 seasonal walks from the *Guardian*
Country Diary by John Gilbey

Country Diary
Wales

GRAFFEG

Contents

Autumn

Winter

John Gilbey

John Gilbey is a writer and photographer based in west Wales. His work has appeared in the *New Scientist*, *Geographical*, *Times Higher Education* and the science journal *Nature*, as well as the *Guardian* newspaper, which publishes the Country Diary column. John has contributed to the column, established back in 1906, since 2006. From his home near Aberystwyth, he sets out to provide a monthly image of the rural landscape across Ceredigion, Powys, Pembrokeshire and Gwynedd. These walks, reached by bus or train and occasionally concluding with a quiet pint, seek to capture the key notes of the season and give others an opportunity to join him on his travels. His career in environmental research, and a lifelong interest in landforms and ecology, give him a solid base on which to build the story of the varied landscapes of Wales.

Left: The Afon Mawddach in autumn.

Introduction

I first came across the Country Diary column of the *Guardian* newspaper forty years ago, during a long winter of unemployment. The local public library, the warmest free venue available, offered access to the newspapers for both job adverts and escapism – which the Diary certainly was. Its tales of moorland, hills and rivers helped distract me from my mundane situation, but to be able to write about the countryside and get it published was still a distant dream.

Thankfully, a variety of jobs followed – but I never quite abandoned the idea of writing for the Country Diary. Eventually, in June 1999, I plucked up the courage to phone the editor. Her assistant suggested I send in an example, which she promised to keep on file in case they ever had a vacancy. I was privately sceptical, but faxed (yes, it was that long ago) 400 words off to them the following morning.

Late one evening in the autumn of 2005, when I'd almost forgotten about it, I had a phone call. It was from Celia Locks, who edited the column at the time, asking if I would like to contribute a Diary. Yes, please! My first column appeared on 28 January 2006, and I am just about to write my hundredth. This collection contains fifty of them, along with some of the photographs I took along the way. It is arranged by season, starting with meteorological spring – March to May – and then following the year around.

I hope you enjoy reading them.

John Gilbey
Aberystwyth, Ceredigion – January 2022.

Wales Map

Places and chapter numbers:

GWYNEDD

Afon Mawddach

Barmouth

Dolgellau

Cadair Idris

Dyfi Estuary

Machynlleth

Aberdyfi

Caersws

Ynyslas

Borth

Talybont

Clarach

Aberystwyth

Comins Coch

Llyn Pendam

Llangurig

POWYS

Llannon

Aberaeron

CEREDIGION

New Quay

Cardigan

Cilgerran

CARMARTHENSHIRE

PEMBROKESHIRE

1. Spring Constitutional

A day of sunshine, after the striking reversals of the weather in recent weeks, is something to be celebrated. Turning my back on the hills, I set out to walk to the coast a few miles distant.

Following days of cold, grey cloud, the injection of colour from the open sky was revelatory – the swelling buds and early catkins giving a hint that maybe, just maybe, winter was on the wane.

Cresting the hill above Aberystwyth opened up a panoramic view across the breadth of Cardigan Bay. I skirted the town along seldom-used paths and reached the sea just below the impressive mass of Constitution Hill. What little wind that remained from the storm was blowing offshore, leaving the sea tranquil and echoing the uneven blue of the sky. Small wavelets, surging and breaking in elegant crescents on the shoreline, reflected the wider story of the conditions far out to sea.

Above the surf-shaped beach of wet cobbles and shingle, the cliffs outlined the ancient, troubled geology of the region. Rocks laid down as muddy sediment under warm, Silurian seas have been crushed and distorted by subsequent movement. Almost vertical planes of rock stand sheer, sunshine highlighting the minerals arrayed within their structure, while arches of twisted strata speak of monumental forces acting over long ages of time.

A column of cloud edged over the sun, cutting the more vibrant colours, and suddenly the scene was returned to winter monotony. I walked south, past the wave-cut rocks where stalwart Victorians took up sea bathing.

Planed almost flat by erosion, they emerge just proud of the beach like the fragmented spines of some ancient beings – which, in a sense, I suppose they are.

Left: Constitution Hill.

Having reached my goal, I faced the long drag back uphill. Just before the landscape reabsorbed the view to the south, I turned and looked down the coast – as I have so often in recent weeks. Increasingly pale and faint as the distance increased, a series of headlands marked out where rural communities lie tight to the shoreline. At the limit of vision, I thought I could just make out the promontory beyond which much of my closest family – unvisited for months because of the pandemic – remains out of reach.

Above: Bath Rocks, Aberystwyth.

2. The Edge of the Roman World

High in the Cambrian mountains of Mid Wales, perched on a slope above the chaotically youthful river Afon Tarenig, the bleak aspect of the Roman fort at Cae Gaer speaks of military expediency and urgent purpose.

In the sunshine of early spring it looks almost serene. But to a newly arrived legionary, in the depths of winter, immersed in an alien landscape still home to wolves and bears, it must have felt like the edge of the world.

Surrounded by steep hills, the location of the fort is an elaborate compromise. Close to fresh water and commanding the junction of two valleys, the site would have forced an enemy to take a long and uncomfortable diversion around it. Every detail of the foe's military life, however, would be visible to a watcher concealed on the slope above.

A roughly square enclosure, the fort was built from turf ramparts topped by a wooden palisade. Nearly twenty centuries later, the banks, densely covered now in heather and coarse tussock grasses, are still surprisingly intact, and the ditches outside them continue to be a significant obstacle to the aspiring visitor. Which, as my companion pointed out, was the whole idea.

Enclosing about a hectare of poor, waterlogged land, the fort is a small, basic structure, perhaps associated with the campaign of Quintus Veranius Nepos in the winter of AD 57.

This newly appointed governor of Britain set out to subdue the intransigent Silures tribe, early masters of guerilla tactics, but didn't survive to complete his task.

I stood close to where the northern gate had been, wondering what it would have been like to stand guard here long ago, perhaps relieved by the news that a mission had been stalled by the death of the governor and that soon we would be pulling back to the new garrison at Viroconium.

Bordered now by bland commercial forestry, the fort endures as a pale pattern in the landscape, briefly visible from the fast, twisting trunk road to the coast. Passed by, in every sense, it lingers as a footnote on a footnote of history.

Right: Ditch and bank, Cae Gaer.

3. History in the Landscape

Between the village of Llanon and the sea lies an area of flat land perhaps a kilometre wide, bordered to north and south by minor rivers.

On the large-scale maps of the area it is labelled Morfa Esgob – which translates roughly as Bishop's Land. In contrast to the steep, thin-soiled hill pastures inland it is a favoured spot. Well drained and quick to warm in spring, thanks to the great heat store of Cardigan Bay, the land is now mostly grazed, but both map and landscape hint at a more complex past.

The tithe map of the local parish, recently digitised and interpreted as part of the Cynefin project, captures a snapshot of the land as it was in the 1840s. It reveals Morfa Esgob as a collection of several hundred interlocking 'slangs' – narrow strips of farmland – each of a size that could be managed by a single household.

Looked at from the ground, many of these are effectively merged into larger fields fenced with posts and wire, but the low winter sunshine reveals subtle banks – evidence of the old alignments.

With scholarly caution, this field system is often termed 'pre-19th century' – the date of the first formal survey. Given that ownership by the church is recorded by the 1300s, however, the strips are almost certainly medieval – and just possibly much older. The turfed footpaths and tracks that give access to the slangs retain their sense of age, hinting at the centuries of daily journeys from homestead to field and back.

Right: Slangs outside the village of Llanon.

There is a still greater timescale at work here. At the seaward edge, erosion is eating back into the slangs, creating a fragile cliff. From the beach below, the profile of water-rounded stones, distinct lenses of clay and a loose matrix of gravel betray the origin of Morfa Esgob as material washed from beneath glacial ice.

Walking back through the neighbouring hamlet of Llansantffraed, it struck me that even the ancient, white-rendered cottages and slate-hung church seemed temporary when judged by the calendar of geology.

....

Above: Erosion shows the history of the landscape.

4. Winter Fights Back

Being west of the mountains, we missed the worst of the recent bout of snow – but the gale-force easterly wind had a significant impact.

Our house, tucked under the shoulder of the hill, is well sheltered from the usual winter winds that roar out of the south-west but the wide, open view of the hills to the east comes at a price.

A sudden ice-laden squall had driven me briefly outside to salvage some tumbling plant pots when the steel cowl was wrenched from the top of the chimney. It missed me by fewer feet than I would have liked and bounded off down the frozen garden with a sound reminiscent of a galvanised bucket being dropped down a flight of stone stairs.

In the aftermath, as we surveyed the damage to plants and property, the wind dropped almost to nothing, leaving a heavy mist hanging over the inland snowfields. When the hillsides emerged into muted sunshine a few days later, all but the highest peaks had begun to thaw, leaving lines of white where ramparts of snow had been heaped against hedgerows by the storm.

As the temperature and light intensity grew, birds that had maintained a discreet profile during the strong winds returned to feed.

Groups of starlings noisily occupied and explored the newly exposed fields, sunlight bringing out the vivid iridescence of their plumage. Tempted outdoors, I trudged up the hill and looked north towards Snowdonia. The dull murk of previous days had been replaced by banks of cumulus cloud and a brilliantly blue sky, the ice-patched profile of Cadair Idris starkly outlined against it.

Crossing the watershed and dropping down into the valley of the Rheidol, signs of the freeze were all but gone. From a distance, the groups of trees dotted along the flood plain showed the slight bright mistiness that colours them just before the leaves finally emerge, accentuated by the low angle of the afternoon sunlight. Lodged under a hawthorn hedge, in so protected a position that at first I took it for a lamb, I came across a final patch of snow. Hopefully this tired, slumped remnant of winter will be the last I will see until year's end.

Left: Snow falling above Comins Coch.

5. Looking North

The narrow lane down to the beach was edged with the yellow flowers of celandines, huddled at the base of the hedge. After days of rain, the field drains jetted water from the steep, saturated fields above, giving the overgrown brook an unusual urgency as it tumbled towards the water-rounded cobbles of the shoreline.

Storm surf driven by recent gale-force winds had stirred up sediment and detritus from the floor of the shallow bay, leaving the seawater discoloured and turbid. Breaking waves still pitched and roared over the dark, outlying skerry rocks and hissed across the wave-cut shallows, while oystercatchers wheeled uncertainly above their usual perches.

The coast path towards Borth, steep and unforgiving as it loops around the scalloped cliffs, climbed muddily between shoulder-high banks of gorse. The stonechats that often sing here were absent, perhaps deterred by the strong wind, but on the hilltop pastures lambs raced in groups around the stolid ewes. They were clearly enjoying the warmth of the sunshine, for what was probably the first time.

At the crest of the path, the view to the north opened up dramatically. A broad line of surf picked out the sweep of the beach towards Ynyslas, while the hills of Gwynedd beyond lay half hidden in cloud and murk. Between the two, the sand-banked and marsh-fringed estuary of the Afon Dyfi reached inland towards Machynlleth.

This spot, Craig yr Wylfa, is well named – translating roughly as the lookout rock. On a good day, you can see the whole breadth of Cardigan Bay from here – a horizon fifty miles across.

....

Left: Borth, with the bog and Dyfi Estuary beyond.

This was not one of those days, but the strategic advantage gained by anyone who held the cliff in historic times was still evident.

Dropping out of the wind, the grassy slope towards Borth gave me time to look across the expanse of Cors Fochno, the great peat wetland beyond the Afon Leri. Beneath towering clouds, the patches of open water within the mosaic of mottled vegetation looked almost black in the afternoon sun, but the light suddenly softened. Glancing westward, I could see the next bank of high cloud begin to obscure the sun. More rain was on the way.

....

Above: Offshore rocks are pounded by the waves.

6. The Sunken Forest

After the long winter, with its numbing cold and sustained snowfall, few things raise the spirits as much as walking under a deep blue sky with the afternoon sun warming your back.

Add to this a long stretch of empty beach and the scope for improvement becomes vanishingly small. My visit to Borth was timed to coincide with a spring tide, whose dramatic range exposes at low water much that is usually covered by a confusion of surf. Winter storms scour the beach dramatically, and a visit in early spring often yields previously hidden elements – including new areas of the ancient sunken forest for which the beach is well known.

Right: The remains of an ancient tree.

The especially low tide revealed a part of the forest I hadn't seen before – a dozen feet or so below the peak high-water mark, stumps of trees and jumbled arrays of prostrate trunks stood out from the scalloped ripples of the beach. Beyond them I could see tangled shallow root systems set in a glossy, eroded matrix of clay and woody peat. Some newly exposed trees had surprisingly well-preserved bark still in place, and several were immediately recognisable as birch. Dated at around 5,000 years old, these trees appear to have lost a battle with rising sea levels after the last ice age.

Welsh legend carries intriguing tales of the lost land of Cantre'r Gwaelod (the Lowland Hundred), a fruitful tract beyond the present shoreline whose sea defences were inundated through either poor maintenance or drunken error.

Could this be a folk memory carried by word of mouth for thousands of years, or is it a later tale devised to account for the same evidence of change visible today? Opinions appear divided, but as I watched the incoming tide gently moving the individual sand grains of the beach it was clear that change is the natural state of the coastline – whether we like it or not.

Right: Trees and their roots in the sunken forest.

7. Falling Water

A narrow-gauge steam railway winds across the steep southern side of the Rheidol valley, slowly climbing the route from Aberystwyth to Devil's Bridge.

While walking deep in the valley beside the river, I was convinced I could hear the train coming and hurried out of the trees to see it pass. The noise persisted, drifting in and out of my hearing as though the engine were rounding the rocky spurs and disappearing into wooded side valleys, yet no train appeared.

Slowly, awkwardly, I realised that the sound was that of the low set of waterfalls further up the valley, distorted and modulated by the strong east wind that was straining the still bare branches of the trees. When I reached the Rheidol falls, having taken the sloping path from

just beyond the old chapel, it was clear that the river was in spate from the recent rains, with substantial volumes of water pouring over and between the rocks.

From the footbridge in front of the falls, the sound of falling water was even more impressive, with a strange pulse that added to the almost hypnotic random noise. In midstream, a series of deep, bowl-shaped pits in a rock outcrop showed the true erosive power of this water. Small imperfections in the stone have been worn deeper, creating voids within which pebbles swirl and scour at times of high flow.

Right: Waterfalls and gorse in the Rheidol valley.

The sun was still high, but the shadow of the valley side already reached out over the narrow fields of lowland pasture. As sheep enthusiastically grazed the tender grass of early spring, a group of six red kites squabbled overhead, pitching and stooping over the conifers nearby. After an extended dispute, all but two moved off, leaving the apparent victors to dive abruptly and perch in one especially tall tree, perhaps a high-status nesting site.

I made a note to return here later in the season and see how they are getting on, but the chill of the wind was becoming insistent and I was keen to get moving again – further inspired by thoughts of tea and cake.

Above: The Afon Rheidol below the falls.
Below: Early spring in the Rheidol valley.

8. A Quiet Morning by the Afon Teifi

It was still early morning when I reached Cilgerran, with the sun too low in the sky to bring much warmth to the deep, wooded valley of the Afon Teifi.

Set in a narrow gorge cut by meltwater during the excesses of glacial times, the river once served as an important resource for the slate quarries that crowded the banks. Shallow barges, on a varied schedule to suit the tides, would load here before travelling the few miles downstream to Aberteifi/Cardigan, where the stone was transhipped into coastal vessels. Today, the quayside and riverside paths are quiet, and for most of my walk I had the valley to myself.

My arrival was clearly not appreciated by a robin, which, singing directly at me from a lichen-covered branch perhaps a dozen feet away, made it obvious that my intrusion was deeply unwelcome. As I walked eastward, the urgent songs of blackbirds and other robins from perches high in the woodland contrasted with the languid sound of slowly churning water and the soft movement of the bare upper branches in the breeze.

Water, running from the steep, moss-covered rock faces, made the path slippery and thick with mud. Beyond the fringe of wood anemones and celandines, the edge of the river was tangled with driftwood and other organic debris, and I found myself looking for signs that otters had passed this way.

I didn't find any definitive prints, but at one spot the vegetation was framed around a gap in the bank that looked well used.

The thick, tangled undergrowth and fallen wood immediately beyond the path would make a quiet spot to lie inconspicuously.

Just below where I stood, slightly upstream of a bend in the river, some quirk of fluid dynamics caused an audible upwelling of the flow. The surface of the water was raised a fraction in a flattened dome, which spun off a line of eddies that slowly filled, like the disturbance caused by the movement of an oar blade. This looked similar to the passage of a submerged animal, but sadly wasn't. Nonetheless, I'm convinced otters were close by, and on a future visit I hope to catch a glimpse of one.

Left: A robin sings in the woods of Cilgerran.
Right: Eddy marks on the surface of the Afon Teifi.

9. Dangerous Currents

Passengers for Morfa Mawddach station, to use the formal language of the announcement, 'should inform the conductor that they wish to alight'.

Your reward, if you do so, is a single narrow platform overlooking the salt marsh on the southern side of the Mawddach Estuary. The station was once an important railway junction and, almost hidden by the undergrowth, an abandoned platform edge marks where a second track curled eastward towards Dolgellau. This line has been closed for more than fifty years, but the trackbed has found a new life as a route for walkers and cyclists.

Following the gentle curve of the trail, engineered for the exacting needs of steam trains, I was steered inland between lines of trees. Wet pasture and fen fell away on both sides of the raised route, and on this cold, grey afternoon only the antics of the newborn lambs brought any movement to the scene.

Near Arthog I turned north alongside the sea wall. Here, glistening mudbanks were marked with the tracks of wading birds while dark water sluiced along deep tidal channels. The path cutting the corner across the fen was wetter than I'd hoped, and those who had walked it before me had braided the route ahead into unattractive, boggy sloughs. As I pondered my options, aware of time passing and the ground yet to cover, I realised that pools of water were forming in the thick carpet of dormant vegetation around my boots.

Right: The south side of the Mawddach Estuary.

Muddy but unbowed, I reached the shoreline rocks near Fegla Fawr and found an old sign I had missed on previous visits. Corroded and tilting slightly, it warned of 'Very Dangerous Currents in Channel Between High & Low Tides' – a form of words that, in my fatigued state, I found oddly perplexing. Does the same risk also occur between low and high tides? And, as high and low water are effectively mere points in time, isn't the danger almost continuous? Today, officialdom would probably say 'Dangerous Currents' and be done with it – leaving a tired old pedant like me with fewer points of argument.

Left: Dangerous currents sign.

10. Visits from the Sparrowhawk

I found the remains of the blackbird on the strip of rough grass between the hedge and a group of small holly trees.

The drift of pale feathers drew my eye first, left in a generous arc where they had fallen after being plucked from the body. Apart from the tail, legs and sternum, little remained of the bird itself, a small adult female, possibly one of those raised in the same hedge last summer. It seemed to have been eaten from the top down, perhaps the same direction from which it had been attacked, and I ran over in my mind the list of possible assailants.

In this quiet, wooded corner my suspicions soon fell on our local sparrowhawk. Only an occasional, solitary visitor to the garden, this hawk has shown an especially messy interest in the growing number of collared doves that frequent the beech trees along the lane. They are almost the perfect prey – large, slow moving and seemingly not very observant – and I have seen them fall victim to the hawk on at least two occasions.

The first time was an early July morning a few years ago. As I opened the curtains to look across the valley, the sparrowhawk was directly below me in the rough grass, just a few yards from where I would find today's blackbird, standing on top of a dove and starting to eat. The window was open and the wooden clunk of the curtain rail made it look up. I stayed perfectly still as we regarded each other – then it took flight and jinked away through the trees, leaving me to literally pick up the pieces.

More recently, at dusk in early October, I was alerted by a heavy impact against the glazed back door. It sounded as though a football had hit it, but the perfectly defined bird-shaped grease mark left on the glass told another story. The sparrowhawk perched briefly on a nearby bench, shaking its head as though stunned, before lurching away, leaving its kill behind. This second collared dove was eventually scavenged by a red kite, as perhaps were the remains of the blackbird. Very little goes to waste in the rural food chain.

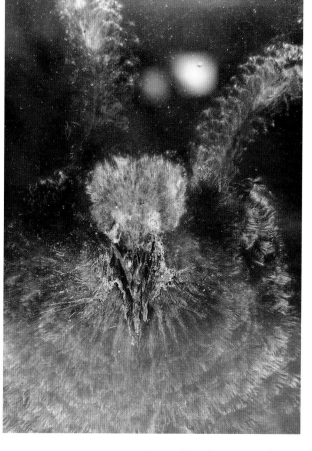

Left: The local sparrowhawk eats a collared dove. *Right:* The greasy print of a bird on the glass back door.

11. Stone Walls and Upland Lambs

My late start meant that the sun was already much further west than I had hoped. The light had moved on from the eastern slopes, and deep shadows lay across the shoulder of Cadair Idris, with the summit outlined in sharp relief against the deep blue of a flawless sky.

I took the lane that runs gently uphill between stolid banks of mossy stone towards a band of low woodland. As I walked, I tried to roughly calculate the mass of the stonework I passed, and before reaching the top of the rise, less than a mile distant, I had accounted for several hundred tonnes.

Most of this would have not been brought far, just prised from the ground and heaped to form boundaries in an attempt to improve the rough grazing either side of the lane. Today, ewes and their small upland lambs grazed unconcernedly among clumps of soft rush as I wandered past in the spring sunshine.

Even in this landscape of rock, and little else, the scale of the effort needed to build these walls is impressive. Yet trees, growing unchecked from the field margin, have heaved the massive blocks aside in places – leaving parts of the structure in a precarious state.

Beyond the crest of the hill, the lane dipped between patches of pleasantly unkempt woodland. Small streams, rock bedded, flowed only gently due to the lack of rain, and the dry moss and lichen that covered the boulders at the margin formed a crisp, matted carpet.

Right: Landscape near Cross Foxes.

Bramble stems as thick as my thumb hung heavily across the walls, already sprouting tight clumps of leaf at their growing points as they wove insidiously across the landscape.

Dropping towards the valley of the Afon Wnion, I found a field gate to lean on while I ate my belated lunch. In the far distance, dimmed slightly by haze, the afternoon sun glinted on the surface of the Mawddach Estuary where the river wound tightly between sandbanks and marshes.

The heat of the day made it tempting to linger, but time was short and, reluctantly, I began the long descent towards Dolgellau.

Left top: Dry stone wall covered with lichen.
Left: Ewe and twin lambs.

12. Beech Woods and Wild Garlic

My route through the beech woods was chosen to avoid the worst of the cold northerly wind that was cutting across the valley. Though the majority of leaves were still to open, the trees broke up the breeze and let me slacken the pace I'd needed to keep warm.

The acoustic of this woodland is softened by its deep, moist leaf litter; outside sounds are dramatically attenuated, letting you focus on the spring birdsong and the occasional creak of high branches stirring in the wind.

Right: Flowering wild garlic overhangs the path.

As I do every year, I was looking for the patches of wild garlic flowers that characterise this season for me. Blooming later here than the primroses and celandines, their flush of white flowers comes just at the point where spring activity goes into overdrive, the unfurling beech leaves splashing colour across the woodland canopy.

The first group of wild garlic plants I came across were still developing, with the flowers sheathed and their white petals just starting to emerge, and I began to wonder whether I had made the trip a week too early. I wandered on, deeper into the wood, noting the way that moss and lichen have begun to colonise the stumps of those trees that were thinned out a few years ago.

Then, turning aside from the main track, I found what I was looking for – a dense layer of firm, curved leaves and flower stems that reached to my ankles almost covered the narrower path ahead.

Moving on further meant brushing against them, releasing the characteristically delicate scent of the spring plant. As the woodland warms and the wild garlic matures, this odour will grow to become fragrant, then strong and eventually overpowering – hanging over the woods like a miasma.

Some like the smell, others endure it. In my own case, the spring scent of *Allium ursinum* never fails to make me feel hungry – and it tends to cling long after you have left the plants behind. A small price to pay for the sight of the frail-looking globes of white flowers that do so much to brighten the floor of the woodland.

••

Right: Wild garlic flower heads.

13. A Hot Day on the Coastal Path

The air was almost still, and only the smallest of ripples marked the edge of the receding tide; the only artificial sound was that of a single boat engine far out to sea.

At the back of the beach, a jumble of boulders lay at the foot of cliffs topped by tangled mature trees newly in leaf. I stuck close to the water on the hard, wet sand, keen to shorten the route around the bay as much as possible.

It was warm, and grew hotter still as I turned inland along the bank of the narrow Afon Llethi. The hedgerows, sheltered by the low hills, were rapidly gaining their bright, full-summer foliage, with violets and bluebells adding abrupt points of brilliance in the shafts of sunlight.

Welcome patches of dappled shade cooled the long climb through the low woodland beyond Cei Bach. Pausing at a familiar gate, I noted how far removed the scene was from the harsh February day I first passed this way decades ago, buffeted by the storm-force winds and bitter, wretched sleet that had roared in from the west.

Above the woods, the route cuts across the steep, open slopes towards Craig Ddu. Rafts of dead bracken still covered much of the rough ground, but stunted hawthorn trees in full leaf and blossom, carved into strangely elongated shapes by the wind from the sea, stood out against the dull brown detritus.

Stonechats called from the cover of gorse bushes, moving quickly away when approached, before circling back around to their preferred perch.

Right: The direction of the prevailing wind is clear.

Against a sky of virtually flawless blue, gulls and an occasional fulmar soared and squabbled, their nest sites happily concealed from the trail and inaccessible to all but the most persistent interloper. The path, edged by orchids, dropped in a series of steep turns towards the waterfalls of the Afon Drywi. Over the years, the passage of countless feet has worn a matrix of elliptical steps in the turf, suggesting the scales of some mythical creature.

Sitting on the warm, smooth turf of the clifftop, surrounded by clumps of sea thrift and the sounds of coast and river, I tried not to recall that I was only halfway to my destination.

Left: Sheltered path across the hillside.

14. Molehills and Lady's Smock

In the pasture beside the lane, dandelions have already set seed, their spherical heads intact and waiting for the right gust of wind to break the seeds free and disperse them across the village like invading paratroopers.

The meadow grasses and wild flowers have grown rapidly in confused abundance, but the crown of the oak tree across the field remains more defined by the framework of branches than by new foliage. Possibly the sudden drop in temperature that preceded the late snow selectively stalled development.

Further uphill the old meadow was marked by fresh molehills among the rushes and the lady's smock, showing where these stolid hunters have been clearing and extending their shallow runs. The activity of their favoured prey, earthworms, is triggered by rising temperature and an attractive level of soil moisture – conditions that have apparently been satisfied.

The shade of the beech woods, fringed with patches of fragrant wild garlic, offered sanctuary from the unexpected heat of the day. Blackbirds crashed and flicked through the dry debris of previous seasons, their progress as they searched for insects sounding much louder than seemed reasonable. In some sheltered spots the beech leaves were just emerging, unfolding and filling out almost as I watched, the new growth looking damp and fragile as it trembled in the slight air movement of the woodland.

A small stream cuts down through the wood in a steep, rocky gully, its sides eroded and occasionally unstable. Despite clambering down with the exaggerated caution of the lone

walker, I still ended up sliding the last few yards towards the plank bridge, my flailing descent arrested by a holly bush that proved both unyielding and impressively sharp.

Looking up from where I lay, I could see that the individual trees forming the canopy of the woodland were merging into a single summer mantle, the beech foliage darkening and the older leaves gaining their mature form. Here, close to the top margin of the woodland, the upper boughs have been severely distorted by exposure to the prevailing south-westerly wind – a stern reminder that the current warm, still weather is something to be savoured rather than taken for granted.

Left: Spring colours in the woodland.
Right: New beech leaves emerging.

15. The Quarry and the Coach Road

Across the valley, the hills have slowly adopted the dusty colours and frayed textures of full summer. Widening patches of pale green meadow stood out across the landscape as the silage was cut, wilted and gathered in the welcome sunshine.

The lack of significant rainfall over the past month has reduced the flow of the stream to a meagre trickle, altering the soundscape of the lane and bringing the background patterns of wind and birdsong into sharper focus. The last of the bluebells, nearly hidden by tall grasses, topped the bank, while the seed heads of dandelions, perfectly mature, waited for a liberating gust of wind. At the top of the track, beyond a field of rushes tall enough to conceal a fox, I took the path across the hill towards the quarry. As I paused to look beyond a gap in the hedge, one of the grazing horses wandered over to check my pockets for potential snacks, leaning its head over my shoulder as if to share the view of the Cambrian mountains.

The tunnel of branches over the track brought cool dappled shade, but just down the hillside the canopy was more open than last year. The savage gales of February had partly toppled two of the shallow-rooted oaks, which now rested uncertainly on their neighbours. In the open arena of the disused quarry, the turf overlying the thin soil was crisp and yellow from drought. The emerging flower spikes of the foxgloves that dot the ground had matured over the few days since my last visit, and wild bees swerved urgently between the newly opened blooms.

Right: The dry paths through the old quarry.

At the end of the old coach road, a right turn would have taken me down to the coast. The temptation was strong, but it has been many weeks since I could justify a walk on the narrow cliff path, and I had to settle for the sea glint on the horizon. With regret I turned left and, clambering over the stile, took the footpath across the top field towards home. By the final gateway, the valley opened out below me under a newly leaden sky. As I dropped into the steep-banked road, the cooling afternoon drew the scent of the first honeysuckle flowers down from the hedgerows.

···

Left: The foxglove spikes are starting to mature.

16. Showers and Deep Shade

The rain, when it finally arrived, began with a mist of light droplets that scarcely reached the ground before evaporating in the dull heat.

As the evening darkened, the temperature dropped sharply and heavy showers delivered substantial rainfall for the first time in many weeks. The air was almost completely still, the only sound the insistent hissing impact of rain on leaves.

By morning, the ground was all but dry once more – but when I took the narrow path between the fields of old meadow, the tall grasses at the base of the hedge, heavy with seed, were lodged and flattened by the overnight rain. Across the valley the field of bare soil, where the sloping pasture has been ploughed and reseeded, stood out darkly against the adjacent mown grassland.

At the foot of the beech wood, the lane was even less frequented than usual. The foliage here has darkened over the last week, the dappled shade much deeper than before. Bluebell and wood anemone flowers have gone, leaving a dark tangle of encroaching stems as ivy and fern weave across the still-dry banks. The invasive, almost indestructible, brambles have already set fruit – hard, green indicators of the wild harvest to come.

Beyond the interlocked canopy of trees, the view of the Rheidol Valley widened out. Leaning for a moment on a field gate, I looked over a landscape rich with hedgerows and mature

trees. Sheep grazed and dozed on the fringes of the pale, rush-patched meadow, a red kite circling silently overhead while bees explored the pale dog rose flowers in the top of the hedge.

Evening brought the return of the rain, with lenses of isolated showers moving across the valley before merging into a homogeneous blur of grey that ate away at the view. The sun was low on the horizon when it cleared, cutting below the level of the cloud and lighting up the hills with clarity and contrast. As the shadows grew, the broad stub of a starkly vivid rainbow appeared briefly in the centre of the scene before fading ahead of the approaching dusk. With the light draining away, a single blackbird sang from the top of the beech tree at the end of the lane.

....

Left : A stub of rainbow appeared on the horizon.
Right: Honeysuckle flowers in the hedgerow.

17. Summer Solstice

Long after midnight, with the temperature well above 20°C and humidity high, I gave up attempting to sleep and checked what the night sky might offer in compensation.

With the moon yet to rise, the village was in darkness, swathed in a murky blanket of haze that all but obscured the mountains to the east. Looking up, a few stars were just visible above the beech trees, whose leaves moved silkily together in the warm wind as though breathing, the only other sounds those of the stream and a few distant sheep.

A brilliant, unmistakable point of light, Venus rose over the Cambrian mountains just before three o'clock, fading in and out of view as it was obscured by the lines of cloud that hung above the horizon. Half an hour later the planet was joined by the moon, a thin, waning crescent against a morning sky now tinged with pink as the twilight grew.

As I watched, a few of our brown long-eared bats swooped low over the hedgerows hunting for a last moth or two before returning to the roost in the loft. A brief shower of rain, enough to cool the air only slightly, rattled the beech leaves before moving off across the valley.

The first of the blackbirds started their morning song as the light became brighter. Other birds began to join in, although many – especially the rooks – were far less tuneful.

The summer solstice, the northern-most apparent position of the sun, was now only minutes away, and the orange glow from below the horizon was far into the north-east. On paper, sunrise was due at seven minutes to five, but this calculation doesn't take the topography of the landscape into account.

Left: Sunrise on the summer solstice.

A few moments 'late', the disk of the sun, framed by trees and a distant wind farm, threw the mountains into harsh silhouette, backed by streamers of brightly coloured cloud.

By the moment of the solstice, at twenty-four minutes past five, the depth of colour was already weakening and the banks of haze were building once more across the valley, the air heavy with the promise of thunder.

· ·

Left: Moonrise on the morning of the summer solstice.

Dolgellau, Gwynedd – 27 June

18. West from Dolgellau

The path by the Afon Wnion was liberally scattered with small branches and twigs still carrying tattered leaves, the debris of the storm the previous night.

The wind had moderated slightly but the flag on St Mary's church still stood out strongly from the pole on the tower. Beyond it, the severe northern flanks of Cadair Idris slid in and out of focus as clouds swept across the mountain, their speed reinforcing my doubts about taking a high-level route alone. Today, I decided, was one for the lowlands – a decision that, coincidentally, allowed time for a cooked breakfast.

Right: Cloud conceals the summit of Cadair Idris.

I followed the river westward, the sound of wind in the oak trees merging with that of water moving past the rounded cobbles of the streambed. As in the other rivers I had crossed that morning, the water level was low, after a period without serious rainfall. The flow was sluggish, the water dark, and swirls of foam moved idly with the current. Tall, mature grasses – heads robust with seed – pressed in from the edges of the path, and foxglove spikes, their open flowers haunted by bees, swung heavily in the breeze. The deep scent of the honeysuckle, tendrils tangled around the low oak foliage, lay in heady swathes across the trail as the heat of the sun began to warm the air. In the tumbledown pasture, wet and stalked by little egrets, flag iris blooms added stabs of bright yellow, while arcs of dog rose carved sharp trajectories up from the overgrown hedges.

The tide was high when I reached the narrow wooden toll bridge at Penmaenpool. As the wind-driven water moved impatiently against the stone bluffs to the west of the bridge I was struck by the similarity of this corner of Wales to the landscape of the southern Lake District. These craggy remnants left after the glaciation of the valley, their close-cropped pasture topped by tight groups of trees, sit hard against the water just like those at the northern end of Windermere. As muddled memories of Cumbria and Cambria flooded in, I enjoyed a satisfying moment of dappled sunshine and warm breeze before heading on towards the coast.

Left: The Mawddach trail follows the old railway line.

19. Sunshine and a Skylark

June is the wrong month to be away from your home patch. After three weeks travelling, I returned to find the landscape very different from the verdant, still-maturing spring countryside I had left, with the darkened, dusty foliage of high summer now firmly in place.

In my absence the tangled, robust hedgerows that bound the lane have thickened further with new growth, the delicate dog roses having grown from bud to full bloom while the honeysuckle flowers built from subtle to strident colour.

Where cattle had been excluded from the pasture, meadow grasses now carried fat seedheads growing pale and dry. In the full sun of early afternoon clover flowers on the point of setting seed bobbed animatedly in the strong breeze.

Weeks in the dry, high rangelands of Colorado and Wyoming had left me with a deep desire for the sights and sounds of the sea, so I headed for the coast path more quickly than I otherwise might have. The thrift flowers in the thin cliff-top turf were bleached and pallid, far from their striking pink when they are newly emerged – but the sturdy, succulent foxglove spikes were brightly and actively blooming.

I stretched out in the smooth-leafed, crisply dry grass near the cliff edge, idly watching a group of jackdaws disputing some minor trophy and listening to the erratic waves of a confused sea break on the rocks below.

Right: Looking north along the coast path.

Invisibly high above me, almost inaudible through the sounds of surf and wind-blown grasses, a skylark began to sing – a tumbling, triumphant song that always brings to mind the summer chalk downlands of my youth.

There were many other things I should have been doing, but none of them seemed as immediately worthwhile. To the west, the sun cast a silver trail across the deep blue of the bay, and I resolved to stay a while longer.

It was still several hours until sunset, and I might yet see seals haul out on the shore, or perhaps a pod of dolphins carve a path across the seascape. I didn't, of course.

....

Left top: Wave-cut platform at the base of the cliff.
Left below: Grasses and sea thrift on the cliff top.

20. Summer on the Afon Leri

Beyond the battered 'No Through Road' sign was a lane I had often passed by, but never explored until now.

It is like many similar tracks on the western side of the Cambrian Mountains: deserted minor roads that serve a few houses and farms, then fade and lose themselves in a tangled web of valleys.

As I followed the road, it narrowed and twisted. Beside it, an array of tall grasses matured at the margin of a steep hay meadow. The only sound was the rising wind surging around the seed-heads and trees. I'd just reached the first gate across the lane when I noticed a path dropping down towards the river. Unfrequented and rich with fresh growth of bramble, the route was defined by substantial stone flags still slippery from the overnight rain. Close to the river, these gave way to massive water-rounded boulders and a narrow footbridge over the Afon Leri.

The water level in the river was low, with sunlight filtering through the newly darkened leaves and falling across the pools and riffles. Several rocks in midstream were flecked with guano where birds had perched; in the hope of seeing a dipper, I settled on a large boulder and let the sounds of the day close around me. In the shaded wood above, blackbirds called and chased in the undergrowth – crashing loudly through the crisp debris of last autumn.

As I waited, my focus closed in on the small group of wet rocks, noting how their positions in the stream forced the flow into ridges of standing water.

The uneven profile of the riverbed added further orders of complexity to the convoluted surface. As I sat perfectly still, the subtle movements in the space immediately around me became exaggerated – beyond these few yards of river bank, nothing seemed to have substance.

Time passed, and the afternoon grew heavy with the threat of thunder, but no dipper appeared. With no human activity to mask them, the almost random sounds of falling water and moving summer foliage filled the narrow valley. Eventually, reluctantly, I hauled myself up and followed the footpath onward along the edge of the wood.

* *

Right: Rocks form the bed of the Afon Leri.

21. Oxbow Lakes on the Afon Rheidol

From the bridge at Glanyravon, the river water had the look of builders' tea – dark brown and slightly sinister – as it sluiced past.

The storm had raised the level of the water by a foot or more, and the bridge piers were rapidly collecting rafts of fresh vegetation dislodged from the banks further upstream. Between the sharp, but thankfully transient, showers, swallows fed low over the river and between the riverside trees.

The recent heavy rain, after weeks of now almost forgotten drought, brought a spell of intense change in the hedgerows and the hazelnuts were rapidly forming – pale and plump. The rich, dark growth of midsummer was taking over from the vivid young leaves of a month ago, and the rains had washed clean the dusty foliage around the honeysuckle flowers – except beneath the buzzard's favourite telephone post, which remained stained with streaks of white.

The lowland course of the Afon Rheidol has moved substantially over time. Across the flood plain, just east of Aberystwyth, oxbow lakes and almost overgrown backwaters show the variety of places the river has been as it has meandered its way across the broad valley floor. The valley sides, steep from the erosion of ice and water, have modest cliffs in a few places where the river has, in the past, wandered right up against them. Here, swampy tracts of woodland surround misfit streams half dammed with moss-covered fallen trees.

Right: Cattle graze in the Rheidol valley.

At Capel Bangor, the gravel island in midstream, shrunken by the rising river, carried foxgloves in full flower, which stood half underwater around its fringe. Recrossing the river, I headed north across the grain of the country through steep, deep-hedged lanes – passing stone built farms and an ancient, somnolent sheepdog which suffered the indignity of not seeing me until it was too late to make a fuss.

Overhead, where the buzzards and red kites circled with an air of mutual suspicion, the thin ribbons of blue sky began to close up as the next wave of rain clouds moved in from the west.

Left: Summer foliage in the Rheidol Valley.

22. A Close Encounter

My route home was badly overgrown and I made slow progress, looking down at the rocky, uneven ground and concentrating on keeping a good foothold.

Bees and small moths swirled up from around the wild flowers and long grass at the base of the hedge, then something much bigger blundered away from under my feet.

The abrupt, jerky flight was a surprise and oddly reminiscent of the tiny hummingbirds of western California – but this was a dramatically more ancient organism. As it rose above the tangled grasses, the wingbeats of this golden-ringed dragonfly (*Cordulegaster boltonii*) were clearly audible as a deep, chitinous drone,

Right: Dragonfly perching at the edge of the path.

the frequency modulating as it repeatedly changed direction. I watched it fly further up the path, expecting it to veer away and be lost to view, but instead it settled again on a tall stem.

Moving even more cautiously, I walked slowly towards the dragonfly – the largest specimen I had seen for several years. As I approached, it oriented itself carefully and began to bask in the warm July sunshine. Dramatically marked with contrasting bands of yellow and black, the slender body was as long as my middle finger and, as the stem moved in the breeze, the complex structure of the wing surface created transient patches of iridescence.

Dragonflies have a family history reaching back hundreds of millions of years, with origins almost as distant as the ancient Silurian rocks I was standing on.

The ancestors that flew in the rich Carboniferous atmosphere must have been an especially impressive sight, with fossil evidence showing a wingspan the length of my arm – the apex aerial predators of their day.

Kneeling awkwardly on the ground, I studied the insect for several minutes, noting the way the bulbous, green-tinged eyes almost joined at the top of the head and how the black pincers of the feet gripped the plant. Then, the breeze blew the stem into my shadow and, alarmed by the sudden change of light, the dragonfly started upwards from its perch. Caught by the rising wind, it whirred away across the meadows towards the dark, still oxbow lakes that mark the meandering former courses of the Afon Rheidol.

Right: Trees form a canopy over the lane.

23. The Heat of the Day

Across the valley, the succession of hills fades into a pale blur of haze as the heat of the day begins to build. The fields at the limit of vision are pale now, dry where the silage has been cut, wilted and gathered, leaving the matrix of deep green trees and hedgerows skeletally prominent.

There is no breeze to relieve the rising temperature, so I travel south along the coast in search of respite – hoping that the great thermal buffer of the sea will cool me down. I pause on the clifftop above Aberarth, looking across the expanse of Cardigan Bay to where the sea and sky merge. Both elements of the scene are an almost uniform blue, made slightly milky by a thin veil of insubstantial cloud. Only the darker, moving surface far offshore gives any real substance to the horizon; the nearly flat calm of the inshore waters leaves a white-sailed yacht with barely enough forward movement to maintain a heading.

At the shoreline itself, the brightness and heat are oppressive, both reflecting harshly upwards from the water surface. The tide is exceptionally low, leaving only a few inches of water in the river mouth. Gulls search without obvious enthusiasm around the weed-covered rocks at the margin of the stream, as the heat haze shimmers over the newly exposed boulders at the harbour entrance. While the coastal path is peaceful, and redolent with the coconut summer scent of the rampant gorse, I quickly begin to crave solid shade – something in short supply on these low cliffs.

Evening brings some relief as a sea breeze begins to build. The temperature is still much higher than seems reasonable, but as I retrace my route northward, the sun lowers through the thickening cloud on the horizon.

Left: A yacht moves across Cardigan Bay.

As I watch, the light on the coastal plain near Llanon fades from golden to blue, the curve of the coast beyond fading once again into mist and half-remembered features. Then, slowly, I carry on – driven by thoughts of chilled beer and the cool of a night-time garden.

....

Top: Sheep graze on the clifftop.
Left: Weed in the harbour at Aberaeron.

24. The Watcher in the Gorse

Even on the open slopes above the cliff, the air was hot and humid, making the steeper sections of the coast path seem more of a trudge than usual. South of Aberaeron, in west Wales, the route was almost deserted – so the sensation of being watched was unexpected.

As I struggled past a tangled mass of gorse, I realised that I was being observed by a stonechat perched on a bracken frond. My plodding approach hadn't alarmed him enough to make him retreat and I realised that at least three others, perhaps a family, were nearby. They exchanged the sharply characteristic calls that sound uncannily like two pebbles being tapped together, and which give the species its name.

The spot I was heading for was further away than I remembered, so it was a relief to clamber down into the narrow valley and rest for a moment on a rock by the stream. The steeply dipping beds of blocky mudstone give an interesting asymmetry to this miniature canyon, with the smooth erosion surface on the southern side countered by jagged exposed strata to the north.

Clumps of thrift have established themselves in cracks between the bands of harder rock, while a diverse selection of lichen has colonised the exposed stone. At the seaward end, the brook feeds a small waterfall, sluicing over the rock step into a sheltered pool perhaps a metre deep, from which a solitary bather – or two if they were good friends – might watch the setting sun.

Barely a dozen metres across, the valley gives the impression of a carefully crafted rock garden and water feature prepared for exhibition at a show.

Thunder clouds began to bubble up inland, eventually blocking the direct sunshine. With regret, I headed north again across slopes swathed in bracken and gorse. From out across Cardigan Bay, a Hercules military transport plane swung idly towards the coast, spooking a group of curlew, which lifted over the cliff edge from the foreshore, their familiar whistles merging with that of the turboprop engines overhead.

* *

Left: A stile on the coast path.
Right: A stonechat watches me from the bracken.

25. The Route Across the Teifi Marshes

Shimmering through a blend of August afternoon heat haze and the swirling movement of reeds in the strong westerly wind, the wild expanse of Teifi Marshes was sunlit and inviting. The flooding tide in the river and the open arc of the sky were uniformly blue, with white fair-weather clouds reflected in the still water of the more protected pools.

Before this area was glaciated, the Afon Teifi appears to have looped south of the narrow gorge it now occupies at Cilgerran. The abandoned route has left a broad, low-lying valley whose sides – clearly cut by a wide, meandering stream – are thick with trees. In the 1880s, the dynamic of the landscape was changed further when the Whitland & Cardigan Railway constructed a causeway of dark, blocky furnace waste across the marshland. This impeded the ingress of seawater and began the evolution of the predominantly freshwater environment visible today.

To the south of the old railway line, which is now a welcome route for those walkers who appreciate dry feet, stands of reed almost encircle areas of open water – the brittle hiss of their stems and seed heads moving against each other blanketing out other sounds. Groups of duck preened and dozed on the low mud banks, while a larger contingent of Canada geese argumentatively cruised the creeks of the main river channel to the north.

Right: The wild expanse of the Teifi marshes.

A flash of blue seen fleetingly in the corner of my eye made me wonder if there was a kingfisher nearby. Although I paused at the spot and waited, I saw nothing else, but another walker asked me later if I had seen one – and, to my chagrin, reported seeing it perching in full view.

Despite the recent rain the blackberries were still hard, small and unripe, but the blackthorn bushes alongside the path were heavily laden.

The sloes were already darkening from green to the deep blue of remembered childhood ink, their skins mottled with a characteristic lighter bloom. As the afternoon heat grew stronger the breeze also strengthened, filling the air with the floating, invasive seeds of the rosebay willowherb. Summer might not yet be over, but the signs of its demise are building rapidly.

···

Above: Geese explore a creek in the Teifi marshes.

26. A Lake in the Hills

East of Penrhyn-coch, the single-track mountain road climbs relentlessly along the spine of the ridge.

As the ground rises, the steep, close-cropped pasture and views of distant windfarms give way to the tightening grip of dank blocks of forestry cut through by gravel tracks. Under the shoulder of Banc y Garn, the road, winding unpredictably around outcrops of rock pitted with heather, emerges on to the open panorama of a high plateau.

Away from the trees, the strong wind from the west was keener than I had expected, flattening tall stands of dry grass and raising short, abrupt wavelets on the surface of Llyn Pendam. In the shallow water close to the margin, long strands of water weed moved just below the surface in sympathy with the waves, creating the impression of a vibrant school of fish. Bright red against the dark of the conifer forest, the berries of a rowan tree worryingly devoid of leaves sent a strong reminder of the advancing year.

Squat clusters of heather plants in vivid flower dotted the open scrub, where trees have been harvested since my last visit. Tree stumps and fence posts alike hosted diverse communities of moss and lichen – some elements threatening to peel from the substrate as the strengthening gale hissed across the landscape. To the east, sunshine cut by the rapidly advancing clouds lit first one then another range of hills in sequence, picking out both familiar features and places I have yet to explore.

Joining a sunken track between steep turf banks, I climbed towards a prospective vantage point. The layers of rock – the edge-grain of the country – beneath my boots dipped at a sharp

angle, providing a securely ridged foothold. Until, turning a corner, I discovered that the way ahead was blocked by a flooded slough in the road.

Dark water from the hillside above had filled the track to an impressive depth, leaving little margin for a diversion. Clearly, earlier walkers had pressed on regardless, leaving deep cuts and smears in the fragile shoulder, but my robust early education on such matters has stayed with me. Trying not to see this frustration as a metaphor for the year so far, I retraced my steps and took another route.

•••

Above: Clouds and sunlight on the hilltops.
Right: Trees and heather at Pendam.

27. A View of the Afon Mawddach

The rising sun is all but obscured by a raft of patchy high cloud, and the mist is slow to clear from the valley floor. North of the Afon Mawddach, almost at the coast, I take a lane that turns sharply uphill.

Once past a scattering of houses, the route follows a narrow valley lined with beech and oak trees, whose canopies weave together to create dank shade. Despite the lack of rain, spring water runs in sheets down the shattered slab of the rock where the lane narrows; the route seems unreasonably steep, and in my memory the lane was much shorter.

The gated footpath I am looking for drops away into the valley between dry stone walls, then climbs again over the shoulder of the next ridge. In the increasing heat, the woodland is sullenly quiet – with only a lone robin providing a vociferous challenge to my approach.

Half-buried by leaf litter, a few stone-bounded steps have been cut to help walkers over the steepest of the terrain, angular rock outcrops offering handholds as I haul myself to the crest.

A hidden side trail brings me to a steep overlook carpeted with flowering heather and overhung with rowan. Below me, the estuary of the Mawddach lies grey and leaden, its surface almost unmarked by movement and reflecting

Right: Heather flowering above the Afon Mawddach.

the patterns of the sky.

To the east, wooded ridges interlock around the river, fading by degrees into the persistent murk. Beyond the Mawddach, the great raw expanses of rock that lead up towards Cadair Idris slip in and out of view as thin streamers of cloud roll across them.

Bees explore the heather flowers around my feet, while clouds of flies begin to chase aggressively around me and my late breakfast. I watch as the tide begins to ebb, unclenching pale fingers of water across the salt march below. A breeze from the sea starts to darken the water, while the falling tide begins to reveal the pattern of sandbanks that weave around the channel. I take a final look across at the mist-bound ridge, then clamber awkwardly down from my rocky perch.

....

Left: Stone steps lead upwards.

28. Counting our Bats

Nearly a century ago, someone bought part of the pasture at the end of the lane and built the house we've lived in for about a quarter of its life. This quiet spot faces east into the Cambrian Mountains and the builder cleverly oriented the house to ensure the best view from the front windows.

The steep pitch of the roof has proved popular with brown long-eared bats (*Plecotus auritus*), a colony of which has shared the house with us for the whole of our tenure. Accessing the loft space through a finger-sized gap between weatherboard and tiles, these intriguing mammals are only a few centimetres long but have ears almost as long as their bodies.

Our loft has become a maternity roost in which they raise their young, emerging at dusk to voraciously scour the surrounding gardens and fields for incautious insects. Moths are especially favoured, and the bats often fly close to lighted windows to pick them off. They return before dawn, and we hear the scratch and skitter of their arrival on the tiles above our heads.

Three or four times each summer, members of the local bat group, stalwarts of environmental survey, assemble in our back garden just after sunset. As we sit on benches sipping mugs of tea, the bats crawl down over the tiles and launch themselves from above the gutter, becoming silhouetted briefly against the darkening sky. Bat detectors make audible their location calls as the bats swoop past to check out their observers.

The counts have been encouraging, with the roost tending to grow at a gentle rate. Occasionally it drops sharply in size before increasing again, suggesting that a portion of the group heads off to form a new colony. On our final count this summer thirty-nine individuals were spotted, close to our best result. Soon, the cold weather of autumn will render them torpid and they will slumber their way through the winter towards spring – a behaviour that I have occasionally envied.

Left: Cloud lit by the setting sun.

Dolgellau, Gwynedd – 27 September

29. Revisiting the Precipice Walk

The minor road from Dolgellau to Llanfachreth was longer – and much steeper – than I remembered, but my increasingly frequent pauses let me study the route in some detail.

Expensively specified, in the manner of old family estates, the road was bordered by impressive dry stone walls and buttressed by solid embankments. Stalwart cottages and farmhouses, dated and monogrammed to celebrate their creation by the Nannau estate in the 1830s and 1840s, hint at the kind of investment few can now dream of.

Cool, early morning mist slowly mutated into a sweltering murk that softened the view of Cadair Idris into a series of interlocked, grey silhouettes. By the time I reached the start of the Precipice Walk, which circles Foel Cynwch and is famed for its views of the Mawddach Estuary, I was convinced I'd chosen the wrong destination.

Stubbornly, I carried on past the walls of rounded stone, deep with moss and lichen, that surround the ancient oak woodland of the estate – utterly still and silent apart from the sharp calls of competing robins.

Out on the open hillside, the heather was beginning to look dowdy and faded. More gallingly, nearly all the whinberries had already gone – leaving just the bright autumn tinges of their leaves for me to enjoy, along with the yellow of the gorse flowers. I walked slowly round to the north side of the hill, trying to find a particular spot. The visibility improved slightly, and as the Barmouth bridge ten miles away began to resolve I scrabbled in my bag for an old photograph.

....

Left: Looking west towards the coast.

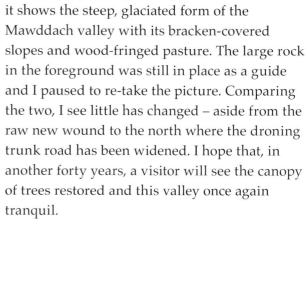

Taken forty years ago on my first visit here, it shows the steep, glaciated form of the Mawddach valley with its bracken-covered slopes and wood-fringed pasture. The large rock in the foreground was still in place as a guide and I paused to re-take the picture. Comparing the two, I see little has changed – aside from the raw new wound to the north where the droning trunk road has been widened. I hope that, in another forty years, a visitor will see the canopy of trees restored and this valley once again tranquil.

Left top: Signpost on the Precipice Walk.
Left below: The narrow path of the Precipice Walk.

30. An Estuary at the End of Summer

Looking across the estuary from the hills above Aberdyfi, the uncertain morning light gave both sea and sky the diffuse grey of long-abandoned pewter.

Behind me, the broken slope of the hillside carried an expanse of bracken fronds – colouring now into autumn. Stirred in the sharpening breeze from the east, they fell into patterns echoing the movement of the river surface below me. The tide had just begun to ebb, with streamers of foam starting to build across the mouth of the Afon Dyfi as increasing volumes of water began to sluice energetically seawards.

Far to the south the notched cliffs of Ceredigion retreated into the coastal murk, while closer at hand the dunes of Ynyslas defined the southern bank of the Dyfi. Caught in a dynamic balance of erosion and deposition, the pattern of dunes is edged to seaward with a ridge of rounded cobbles – visible as a grey band even from here, a mile or so distant. Beyond the sand dunes the great expanse of Cors Fochno, an impressive raised peat bog with its core still virtually wild, brought further diversity of colour and texture to the landscape. A line of silver, oddly straight in this almost fractal scene, marked the engineered course of the Afon Leri across the edge of the mire.

The track across the hillside, edged with gorse flowers and a few late foxgloves, took me down towards the town, finally reached by a half-remembered path dropping between high hedges.

The day had begun to warm, burning away the earlier mist and bringing solid colour to the landscape. Inland, the former mere suggestion of high ground resolved into familiar hills, framed by a deepening blue sky and fans of high white cloud.

As I headed eastwards towards Machynlleth, sunlight reflected sharply from the choppy waters of the Dyfi, throwing into silhouette a good-sized flock of oystercatchers strung out along the widening foreshore. I lost count at 50, which was perhaps a quarter of the group, and was glad to note that this throng included a number of paler, slightly scruffy, juvenile birds. A healthy presence, but the gathering of flocks in the estuary is a sign of approaching autumn that can no longer be ignored.

••

Left: Aberdyfi.
Right: Looking south across the Dyfi Estuary.

···

31. Crossing the Bridge

I have used the bridge across the mouth of the Afon Mawddach many times, but probably haven't given it the attention it deserves.

Usually, arriving here marks the end of the long walk down the estuary from Dolgellau and I have been pushing for a feast of vinegar-soaked chips while waiting for my train home, or to seek a pint and a warm fire, depending on the weather. This time, I made the bridge itself my destination.

This venerable structure was built mostly from heavy baulks of timber, but has an arched iron span at the northern end, which once swung open to allow the passage of shipping. It carries both the single track of the Cambrian Coast railway line and a wooden deck that provides a short cut for walkers or cyclists who wish to avoid the much longer journey via Penmaenpool.

This is a route that should be celebrated, as it forms an important link in the Wales Coast Path, but pedestrian access is reportedly at risk from suggested budget cuts.

In the middle of the almost kilometre-long bridge I stopped and examined the view eastward, while the welcome if unexpected sunshine warmed my back. Close at hand, the mixed woodland on the whale-back mound of Fegla Fawr was showing just the first tinges of autumn colour.

···

Right: The mouth of the Afon Mawddach.

Above the woods of Arthog, the fading heather flowers and bracken fronds on the hillside had started to merge towards a common light russet – cut through with grey outcrops and the occasional bright green patch of improved grassland, divided by pale dry stone walls. Higher still, the scree slopes and the dramatic buttressed ridge that runs towards Cadair Idris loomed into the base of the cloud.

As I turned north again, I looked over the parapet into the blue, opalescent water that the ebb tide was swirling seawards. In the pale, shallower water beside the beds of seaweed, in the shadow of the bridge, a large jellyfish pulsed languidly in the fast-moving flow – just about able to control its orientation, if not its ultimate destination. I know how it felt.

· ·

Left: Looking south across the Mawddach bridge.

32. Sarn Gynfelyn – Folklore and Landscape

Drifts of dry beech leaves from last autumn still edged the stone steps in the woods above Llangorwen.

Strong winds earlier in the week had brought down circles of acorns beneath the oaks, and they popped freshly underfoot. The leaves of the horse chestnuts were starting to gather patches of richer colour, while the spines on the conkers still felt soft to the touch and had so far escaped collection.

The hedges of the lane still held a few honeysuckle and red campion flowers, although the sloes in their white bloom had already passed their prime. The old stone track that runs down to the coast was deserted apart from a couple of fiercely combatant robins. Here, the elderberries looked in perfect form – rich, dark and with the stalks picked out brightly in red.

Following the south side of the valley, and almost roofed over by trees in places, the track opens out beside the overgrown stream onto the shore at Wallog. The fine stone house, the arched lime kiln on the shoreline and the robust sea wall spell out the prosperous past of the area – when coastal craft grounded here between tides and unloaded the limestone which, when processed, would help feed the bitter upland soil.

The most impressive feature, however, is the great pebble bank that juts out into the sea from here. Sarn Gynfelyn, a narrow spur of rounded cobbles, extends more than five miles out into the bay – although only the first few hundred feet are visible. 'Sarn' can be translated from the Welsh as causeway – a hint at the lore which speaks of ancient sunken lands. Logic dictates

that this is morainic material once entrained within a westward flowing glacier – but even on a still, sunny day at the end of summer the sense of a built structure was hard to shake.

From the high point of the cliff path, the curved tail of Sarn Gynfelyn was marked in a darker blue by the movement of the water. To the south I could just see Cemaes Head, while northward the long sweep of the Lleyn peninsula was visible as a series of isolated hills – a view over forty miles wide.

I stood for a while enjoying the sun and the luxury of a place without any man-made sound, but the dark band of cloud moving in from the south-west suggested emphatically that I had chosen the right day to celebrate the end of summer.

....

Left: The glacial feature of Sarn Gynfelyn.
Right: Sarn Gynfelyn extends seaward at low tide.

Dolgellau, Gwynedd – 22 October

33. An Early Walk
from Cross Foxes

The sun was still below the horizon when I left the village, the sky a cloudless blue graduated towards red, and it was only just above the hills when I reached Cadair Idris.

The car park at the top of the pass was already full of folk keen to take advantage of the fine day, which promised to be the last for some time. Balking at the prospect of so much company, I carried on a few miles to Cross Foxes to test a route I'd passed several times but never explored.

At this height, the breeze was stronger than I'd expected, moving the branches that overhung the lane to Tabor and sending the first dry leaves of autumn swirling into shallow drifts. The narrow road, bounded by banks and dry stone walls, rose gently along the shoulder of the hill – opening up the view of a rank of barren, unforgiving ridges. A thin mist still lay across the slopes, insubstantial but most visible where the rising sun created a sharp line of shadow across it. Areas of pale rush and rough grass stood out against the dark green of the cropped meadows, while on the higher land the senescing bracken fronds added a deep, rusty orange to the soft range of colours.

A sudden gust of wind sent a shower of crab apples, conker-sized and hard, rattling onto the lane to bounce and roll a surprising distance before fetching up against a bank. Some of the older, slightly softer fruit showed signs of bird attack, and I wondered whether the pair of jays I saw swooping across the edge of the woods nearby might have been responsible.

The woodland, with the noise of the wind limited to the canopy overhead, was still and dank. Boulders and pieces of stone wall were covered with a continuous layer of moss, rather

....

Left: Cadair Idris from above Cross Foxes.

than the mosaic of lichen on the more exposed walls. Past the old Quaker meeting house, the road begins to drop away. In the distance a corner of the Mawddach Estuary, deep blue in the morning sunshine, illustrated just how far

I still had to walk. I headed on down the long hill towards Dolgellau, and breakfast.

• •

Above: Autumn colours in the landscape.

34. Tribute and Tributaries

Long before the Romans built their two forts at Caersws, the ridge to the west of the town was dominated by the ramparts of Cefn Carnedd. In the low afternoon sunshine the defensive banks that still rise above the hillside woodland were picked out by deep shadows.

The Iron Age fortress stands above a kempt farmed landscape drained by the Afon Hafren (River Severn) as it meanders across the valley floor. Only a few miles from where it rises, gathering volume from the tributary streams funnelling in from the many side valleys, it has already changed from a lively moorland torrent to a broad, stately river in comfortable middle age.

The Severn Way, a long-distance trail that tracks the river from source to sea, follows the break of slope between the north side of the flood plain and the steep woods of the valley side.

Water filtering down the hill had collected in the muddy sloughs of the path, making progress difficult, but after days of gale-force winds, the welcome gentle breeze was just enough to move the seedheads of the rushes bordering the route.

On this quiet autumn weekday I was the only traveller on the path, and to judge from the startled reaction of pheasants and rabbits alike it was little frequented in this season.

Low over the wet grassland a solitary heron beat purposefully along with slow flaps of its broad wings, while high above a buzzard soared idly, gazing with obvious attention at the ground below – occasionally stooping sharply as it spotted an item of potential interest.

The wind began to pick up as the afternoon wore on, lifting dry oak leaves in short-lived vortices and starting to move the larger branches. Long lines of cloud, picked out in evening colours, advanced from the south-west and a new chill came to the shade of the woodland.

Looking at the map, I measured my progress against the distance to my destination and realised I had lingered too long. Setting a new pace, I headed off, determined not to be further distracted.

Left: The floodplain near Caersws.
Right: The Afon Hafren.

35. Marshes and Sandbanks

From my vantage point on the southern side of the Dyfi Estuary it was clear that my plan for the day had been compromised.

The salt marsh, with its almost fractally complex pattern of creeks, pools and drains, is often host in late autumn to large groups of geese grazing contentedly within easy reach of the seawall.

On this visit those few geese visible through the pervasive anticyclonic murk were strung out along the seaward edge of the marsh, distant and difficult to approach. As if in compensation, a single egret, starkly white against the muted greys and browns of the saltings, flapped slowly up from the bed of a creek just in front of me.

Hoping for a break in the gloomy weather, I moved on to Dovey Junction, one of the more remote railway stations in the UK. Perched by the River Dyfi and reachable only on foot or by bike along a gravel track, it gives access to a dramatic rail route along the north side of the estuary.

Across the river bridge, with its lonely cottage, the line follows a rocky foreshore edged with current-sculpted sandbanks where the main channel cuts close to the shore. On this day scattered groups of large jellyfish lay stranded near the high-water mark, oystercatchers scavenged and probed at the edge of the rising tide and ducks formed sociable rafts midstream. But no more geese were visible.

Right: Mudflats are exposed as the tide falls.

The village of Aberdyfi marks the boundary between the river and sea, and even stepping from the train on to its single station platform I could hear the roar of the surf breaking on the sandbar at the mouth of the Dyfi.

Warm sunshine broke through briefly, and from the jetty behind the lifeboat station children fished for crabs – dropping them into buckets of seaweed and water as generations have done before them.

As the sea breeze began to pick up and the shadows lost their definition I looked inland. Fresh masses of grey cloud were starting to drag across the hills of Ceredigion while a solitary cormorant dived repeatedly and with limited success among the moored fishing boats.

....

Left: A boat moored at the mouth of the Dyfi Estuary.

36. From Llanilar to the Coast

The second gale of the week came roaring in off the hills just after dark, bringing down more leaves and small branches from the oaks and beeches.

By dawn the wind had dropped considerably and by the time I reached Llanilar, a few miles to the south, it had gone. Taking the lane past the low stone tower of the church of St Hilary, I walked down to the bank of the Ystwyth, aiming to follow its course to the sea as closely as possible.

The river was not as high as I had expected, and the pebble bank above the weir was still exposed. I searched for signs of otters on the sand at the water's edge but, sadly, none of the prints had enough toes – five – to qualify.

Walking westward, I followed the route of the old railway line, which began life in the 1860s as the Milford & Manchester Railway and was closed 100 years later. The valley opened out to reveal the deep, saturated colours – from green to dark orange – of the woodland on the hillsides.

Crossing the river at Pont Pant-mawr, I took the track up into the lichen-covered, deciduous woodland of Coed Tyllwyd. Recently fallen chestnut cases covered the path at one point but, sadly, they were empty.

Beyond Llanfarian the route rejoins the old railway line. Passing the river's last deeply incised meanders, I entered a dank, wooded cutting and emerged with a startling view of Pendinas, a substantial domed hill, and its Iron Age fort.

Nearing the coast, the dominant sound was
the boom of the storm surf on the great bank of
Tanyblwch beach. The sunshine was weakened
by clouds building up to the south and a fine
salt spray was softening the outline of the coast.
The best of the day was over and as I stood
at Aberystwyth's harbour mouth, where the
Ystwyth empties into the sea, a light drizzle
began to fall.

••

Right: A meander on the Afon Ystwyth.

37. The Autumn Landscape of the Dunes

It was almost low water when I arrived on the southern edge of the Dyfi Estuary. The receding tide had exposed expanses of hard, rippled sand beyond the line of the saltings, while the river itself was reduced to a deep, tortuous channel.

Inland, the landscape was softened by a thin cloak of mist, rendering the southern hills in a palette of blue and grey hues that gave them an oddly two-dimensional appearance, as though the hills were giant pieces of stage scenery stacked together.

The sun was still behind the hills but the broad banners of cloud across the eastern horizon slowly began to brighten and gather a warm glow. I turned west and headed over the wet, compacted sand towards Ynyslas – its semi-stable sand dunes help protect this delicate estuarine system.

Approached from inland, the dunes appear almost permanent, with a closely cropped turf covering the lower, damper areas – a turf maintained largely by the significant rabbit population, to judge from the extent of both droppings and burrows.

A cold breeze began to build as I walked and the sense of autumn was reinforced by the number of fungal fruiting bodies emerging from the sward. I continued seaward and was near the top of the dune system when sunlight suddenly flooded the landscape. The effect was dramatic, with the colours shifting almost instantly from drab to fully saturated so that even the clumps of dry marram grass that help anchor the dunes looked fresh and vital. At the crest, the sound of the waves breaking below was mixed with a lower roar from farther away, where surf broke on the shoal at the mouth of the estuary. The offshore breeze, still strengthening, whipped

Left: Misty hills just after sunrise.

the foam from each breaking wave and carried it seawards. Impressive – but much too cold to linger long.

Above: Early morning light on the dunes of Ynyslas.

38. Paths Less Travelled

The old lead mine at Allt-y-crib, which once spread across the hillside a short walk from the village of Talybont, has been abandoned for almost a hundred years.

Much of the site is now covered with mixed woodland, but several large heaps of spoil are still visible from across the valley. These barren mounds of rock waste, still free from vegetation, are a memorial to the industry that dominated the economy of this area for many decades.

From the base of the woods, the path rose gently westward across the valley side, but became much less distinct as I approached the crest of the slope. Here, saplings grew unchecked in the middle of the path and rotted fallen trunks made progress slow and awkward. Later I realised that I had, not for the first time, taken a less favoured route when a much better one existed nearby.

The footpath across the wet grassland of the plateau beyond was unfrequented, judging by the cobwebs spun across the stiles and the reactions of surprise from the Welsh Black cattle I encountered. Deep grass and a rising breeze made my passage almost silent; in one marshy spot, dotted with soft rush, a snipe abruptly took flight right at my feet – curving away while its alarm call echoed back from the edge of the wood.

As I moved further west, the view of the Dyfi Estuary began to open out. Far to the north-east, banks of cloud gathered over the hills toward Cadair Idris – but I still stood in full sunshine, the warmth of the afternoon light saturating the colours of the remaining oak leaves. Below the

north-facing pasture and autumn hedgerows, the low expanse of Cors Fochno – labelled 'The Great Bog' on historic maps – stood stark and uncompromising. While drainage and agriculture have chipped away at the edges of this wilderness over the centuries, a core of near natural raised bog remains at its centre.

As I traversed the corner of the fen on my approach to the coast at Borth, the wind became colder and more insistent, rippling the surface of the Afon Leri – wider but less youthful than at Talybont – as I crossed it for the second time that day.

Left top: Sunlight through hedgerow trees.
Left bottom: The Afon Leri.
Right: Autumn fields near Talybont.

Aberystwyth, Ceredigion – 6 December

39. Immersed in the Weather

The overnight storm has battered the landscape and torn the remaining leaves from the beech trees, with only a few small oaks maintaining a grip on their senescent foliage.

Frost followed by heavy rain has reduced much of the leaf litter in the lane to a rutted mulch, which deadens the sound of my footfall as I head towards the coast.

Away from the dubious shelter of the hills, I realise just how strong the northerly wind still is, raising short, angry waves even in the sheltered waters at the mouth of the Afon Rheidol. Plumes of beech leaves swirl in the confluence of waters at the harbour mouth; a line of foam marks the margin of the salt water.

In mid stream, a lone cormorant stands on a bank of shingle in apparent defiance as the wind tugs at its plumage, iridescent in the late afternoon sunshine.

South of the harbour entrance, the bank of large cobbles at the back of the beach blocks some wind, but as I climb over its crest I am forced back by the raw pressure of the gale. Flecks of foam, torn from the confusion of breaking waves around the harbour wall, whip up like driven snow around the curve of the bay. Groups of seabirds fly low, tight to the water, seeking shelter upriver.

I clamber southward over the stones, a stronger gust nearly parting me from my hat, while banks of cloud send lines of shadow across the sea and split the sunshine into shards of light.

Right: Light rays fall across Cardigan Bay.

The cliffs ahead of me begin to be outlined with mist and spray from the breaking waves. Heavier cloud, almost fully obscuring the sun, begins to drain colour from the scene, leaving the landscape feeling even colder.

Chilled to the bone, I take a final look across the bay, where the last band of light highlights the coast beyond Aberaeron, and turn back towards shelter. Heading directly into the wind, I bury my hands in my pockets and consider where I might find both beer and an open fire.

Left top: A cormorant stands on a shoal in midstream.
Left bottom: Storm waves batter the harbour wall.

40. New Directions

A village wedding is always an occasion and draws folk back who have long since left to find their place in the wider world.

At the reception I sat with several of the people my children went to school with. Though they are now long adult, I still carry a mental image of them as the band of youthful adventurers who explored the local countryside on bikes in the long summers of memory.

I'd hoped to hear stories of their new lives in places from London to Japan, but they wanted to discuss the things that have happened in the village since they left.

They spoke of the accumulation of small, incremental alterations that have grown – almost unremarked – into greater changes. Housing development where the Victorian school used to be, the growth of the trees by its replacement, the paving of the lane by the stone cottage that generations of children have insisted is haunted, of who is still here, and who – sadly – has passed.

Somehow, a December wedding seems to highlight the start of a new cycle of life much as the approach of the solstice does for the natural world. Walking the village footpaths the following day I noticed afresh the range of interlocking lifetimes, some lived at wildly different paces. The old school is gone, but the hawthorn-hedged path that served it for a century remains – still guarded by the iron kissing gate.

Beyond it, some sheltered beech trees retained a pale selection of leaves from the past summer, while the bulk of fallen material lay as a damp, fermenting mulch on the soil below. The skeletal

crowns of the oak trees, dormant and waiting for spring, described almost fractal patterns across the grey winter sky. In the distance, against a backdrop of ancient mountains, the rain-swollen Afon Rheidol wandered through a landscape that has probably changed little in human memory.

I wandered back through a dusk scented with wood smoke and raised a glass to the health and future of the bride and groom.

••

Above: Holly with berries.
Right: The curve of the lane.

41. Two Rivers and a Puzzle

Deep in the valley of the Afon Rheidol the air was still and cold, heightening the sound of the water moving under the footbridge.

It curled and eddied around the piers of the bridge, with small rafts of foam being captured, released and caught again by the flow. It took me a moment to realise why this picture seemed so familiar, then memory took me to another river, another life and a very different time.

In the early 90s, I cycled to work over the ancient humpback bridge at Pecketsford in Devon, often pausing to look over the low parapet at the curve of the young River Taw where it winds down from the hills of Dartmoor. One bitter February, ice began to form along the fringes of the river,

merging with the snow on the banks. Across the slow, wide eddy in the pool above the bridge more ice began to accumulate, building slowly over the days and nights into a disc several metres across.

Sitting within a thickening arm of ice bound to the eastern bank, this perfect circle rotated several times a minute in the flow of the river, accompanied by the murmur of water gently upwelling in the space between disc and socket. It was an impressive sight, and remained so for several weeks before the inevitable thaw weakened the restraining ice and the disc, shooting the bridge, grounded on the rocks beyond where it lay wedged at an angle like a crashed alien spacecraft.

Right: The Afon Rheidol near Llanbadarn Fawr.

My head full of memories, I walked slowly up the long hill homeward. I took the narrow path between two fields and saw someone coming towards me in the deepening dusk. Not wanting to surprise them, I clicked on my torch. There was nobody there. After a moment's thought I turned off the torch; the 'figure' returned. When I moved, it moved; when I stopped, it stopped. Examining the scene with more logic than I felt, I realised that the remaining light from the sky was creating pools of deeper shadow under the overhanging trees, causing the pale gravelled track beyond to simulate a person. Reassured but shaken, I promised myself a stiff drink when I got home.

· ·

Left: Ice disk on the River Taw at Pecketsford.

42. Sitting Tenant

We inherited the old garden shed when we bought the house a quarter of a century ago.

Over the door, someone had fixed an open-fronted nest box of the type thought suitable for a robin but, whether it was too exposed or the aspect was wrong, no birds took up the offer of accommodation. Eventually, while repainting the shed, I took down the box and, for want of anywhere else to put it, left it on a high shelf just inside the door. That winter, the apple tree nearby lost a branch, breaking the shed window and adding another line to the list of jobs I would never get around to.

Right: Robin in a holly bush with snow.

The following spring, while easing the lawnmower out of its hibernation, I heard an unexpected sound. Turning slowly round, I was met with the attentive but apparently unconcerned gaze of a brooding robin, who had decided that the new location and accessibility made the nest box suddenly desirable. I crept away as quietly as I could, but kept a close eye on the progress of our tenants. The sitting bird received regular deliveries of insects from its mate and seldom left the nest before the eggs hatched.

Once the nestlings were heard, however, both parents kept up a constant shuttle during daylight to try to appease the growing chicks. I am pleased to say that all six youngsters fledged successfully and spread out across the garden while their mottled feathers matured.

While trying to arrest the collapse of the shed this year, I realised that I was patching sections that I'd previously repaired, and a fatal cocktail of rot and gales forced the conclusion that a new shed was needed. The recently completed replacement, sturdily built from robust timbers, should last at least as long – especially since I've significantly pruned the apple tree. For now, the nest box has been returned to an outdoor location, where it is sheltered but still accessible. Hopefully, another generation of robins will come across it in the spring and find that it meets their needs. If they don't, I'll need to find a more creative solution.

●●

Left: Robin perched in falling snow.
Right: Robin nesting in shed.

43. Draining the Landscape

A thick, cold mist hanging in the air gave the breeze a harsh, raw edge. While the rain had stopped, however briefly, the heavy soil was wet beyond capacity and the grass of the pasture stood above terraced pools of muddy water.

A product of glacial times, the boulder clay that lurks below the turf is made up of the irregular geological material swept along by the ice and then deposited in rough aggregations. While almost impervious to drought, the resulting soil is slick and unforgiving when wet, a cloying morass that sucks at your boots.

As I walked up the lane, the sound of falling water was everywhere, as trickling threads of run-off flowing across the fields merged into

deeper runnels and plunged down into the brook beside the path.

For this rainwater, the route to the sea is short but tortuous. The ice sheets that created the debris of rock and clay also blocked the scheme of streams and rivers that existed before glaciation. A great tongue of ice, extending across the shallow valley that would become Cardigan Bay, prevented meltwater draining to the west as the climate warmed. Lakes increasingly filled the blocked valleys until the lines of hills between them were overtopped, and rapid, tumultuous erosion cut new channels towards sea level.

Once the ice sheets finally retreated, much of the old drainage pattern was more or less restored, apart from a few odd corners like the valley spread out below me.

Right: The stream at the side of the lane.

Massive flows of water as the world thawed opened a channel almost a mile wide between this ridge and the foothills of the Cambrian mountains, yet today, the only river in this valley is a quiet stream less than ten feet wide. A quirk of the landscape carries it northwards through this cut in the hills before the misfit river turns west to reach the sea at Clarach a mile or two further on.

Having flowed along almost three sides of a square, the watercourse meets a humble end as a collection of channels flowing through, and across, the curve of the beach. The water-rounded pebbles that form this final barrier are themselves largely of glacial origin, another hint at the overwhelming scale of these events.

....

Left: Steps up to the stile.

44. Through the Gate

The hills in the distance were still banked with snow, but on the narrow path above the village the frost had melted even in the hollows.

At the far end, a rusted iron gate guarded the steps down to the road; pushing it open, I wondered how many times it has swung on these simple hinges, giving access to both school and chapel in the village.

In the wood above the lane, thin shafts of watery sunlight sliced between the limbs of dormant beech trees. Beyond, the crown of the great oak tree stood naked against the sky – each twig, branch and bough utterly still on this windless morning. The loudest sound, aside from the occasional sharp mewing call of a red kite, was that of water gurgling from field drains into the ditch at the side of the road.

I turned north and took the footpath that zigzags across the hillside. Following hedgerows and occasionally diving through copses, the path led me past spots that I hadn't seen in winter for years. A narrow strip of land between fences, once optimistically planted with staked saplings, was now all but bare. Only a single stunted beech tree had survived predation – probably by rabbits, whose tracks through the grasses suggested a robust population.

Fallen wood, sodden and rotting, lay in the undergrowth, made colourful by the rosette-like fruiting bodies of the fungi that were slowly breaking it down. The back wall of a small quarry, long abandoned and eroded by rain and frost, had fallen away from the roots of an ivy-covered tree, leaving it vulnerable and exposed. Slow but significant, the changes have mounted up.

Clambering across the narrow footbridge, I remembered why I avoid this route in winter. For perhaps fifty yards, the path, constrained by the river on one side and a fence on the other, was more than ankle-deep in mud. I traversed it with exaggerated care, just about avoiding a spectacular debacle, and with a sense of relief turned on to the old coach road towards home. Cutting across the top field, I climbed over the final stile – holding on to the narrow, holly-shrouded stone post that probably predates most of the village. Long may it remain.

Left: A frost in the Rheidol Valley.

Machynlleth, Powys – 29 January

45. The Roman Steps

In the fields west of Machynlleth, an old path leads across the hillside towards a notch in the skyline.

Just where it leaves the valley floor, turning sharply to accommodate the steep slope, a set of steps has been carved into the solid rock to aid those following the route. This modest landmark, showing a degree of skill in its construction, is known as the 'Roman Steps' – often in quotation marks to indicate the slightly dubious nature of that claim.

The Romans certainly spent time in the area – the remains of a small Roman auxiliary fort at Cefn Caer, Pennal, lie only a few miles to the west – so it is possible that the feature dates from that time. Alternatively, the name of a nearby field, Cae Gybi, suggests an association with Cybi, a sixth-century saint who was active in north Wales and may well have had influence here.

More likely is that the steps were cut by workers at the long-disused quarry to get to the top of the workings. The hummocks and pits of their endeavours there are still visible, softened by turf and bracken. Whichever mix of origins is correct, the twenty-seven carved steps – or twenty-nine, depending how you count them – stand as a record of rural ingenuity. Although worn, their monumental nature remains, as does the cleverly engineered integral gutter that keeps water from the fields above clear of the path.

Since my last visit, the trees that formed a canopy – almost a tunnel – over the path have been cut back, while uphill of the steps the trail has been graded and surfaced with broken stone. Some of the outcrops that marked the route have been cut away, leaving shards of

....

Left: The Roman Steps near Machynlleth.

rock in raw heaps to one side. I picked a lump of quartz from the spoil, rinsing it clean in a pool of rainwater. Newly scoured from the ground, the white crystalline structure was sharp and unweathered, seeing daylight for the first time since it was formed.

Change inevitably continues, rock will erode, the trees will regrow, but we need to guard humble aspects of our heritage, such as this path.

••

Above: Looking north from the top of the Roman Steps.

....

46. A Winter Climb

The weather looked untrustworthy at best, and it was clear from the outset that our ascent of Cadair Idris was unlikely to be complete.

From the avenue of trees that forms the approach to the Minffordd path, the summit itself is hidden by the steep sides of the glaciated valley, but cloud loomed ominously over the crags of Moelfryn.

Deep in the valley, the air was still and bitterly cold. The only sound was the almost random roar of falling water, as the Nant Cadair – swollen by meltwater – sluiced over the rocks into the deep, clear pools that look so tempting in warmer weather. Deep moss and clumps of fern cling to the stone walls and boulders in the oak wood, moderating the sound and wrapping the walker in a soft acoustic cocoon.

A friend already on his return journey passed us, reporting that some snow remained from the recent fall, and as we left the top of the wood isolated pockets of icy residue began to appear. Looking south across the valley, the contrast between the fertile pasture of the valley floor and the pale, rank grass of the steeper ground was clear. Farming here once relied on a *hafod* – a summer dwelling – in the hills, where you took your livestock for the warmest months, leaving the lowland fields for a hay crop and some autumn grazing. A hard lifestyle, and undoubtedly less romantic than it sounds.

As we climbed into the base of the cloud, picking our way among the twisted moraines left by the glacier that carved this landscape, the patches of snow became larger and more frequent.

The visibility continued to fall and the path became a stream in its own right, so there was little argument when I suggested that the late hour and dimming light made retreat the sensible option. We'll return in a few months, when the spring flowers begin to emerge and the rocky bulk of the mountain is again framed by a deep blue sky reflected in the still waters of Llyn Cau.

Left: Rocky stream on Cadair Idris.
Right: The path leads up into the clouds.

Snowdonia – 16 February

47. Ice and Sunshine

There was a thick layer of frost on the wooden sleepers of the railway crossing as I carefully made my way over the track.

The long ridge above Pennal carried a crust of snow that drew rock outcrops into sharp relief, usually concealed by random vegetation but now looking skeletal and exposed. On the valley floor, mist rose gently from small groups of sheep that clustered together in the morning sunshine.

As I crossed the col above Corris, the main peak of Cadair Idris came into view, its striking snow cover outlined by deep blue sky and supported by the dark browns and greens of the Minffordd woodlands. The snow extended down the flanks of the mountain as far as the corrie lake of Llyn Cau, about 1,500ft above sea level, picking out the rock step over which the ice once poured into the valley glacier – much easier to picture in these winter conditions. Steep, south-facing rock buttresses, having shed their snow cover, stood out against the frosted bands of scree that edge downwards towards the pass.

A few miles farther north on the shore of the Mawddach Estuary, fractured sheets of ice stranded by the falling tide lay in angular shards on the mudflats. Drifts of wood smoke from the fires of isolated houses rose almost vertically into the still air, while the surface of the water was disturbed only by the hopeful foraging of gulls. The loudest nearby sound was that of a small stream falling over a steep stone bank.

· ·

Left: Snow covers the summit of Cadair Idris.

Spray from the waterfall had thickly glazed the bushes to one side in brilliantly clear ice, with secondary icicles hanging from the twigs to form a complex lattice.

Only a few days later, the snow and blue sky have gone, the temperature has risen by ten degrees and a monochrome, drizzly murk covers a landscape suddenly almost devoid of features. To be honest, I preferred the frost.

....

Left: Ice-covered plants by a waterfall.

48. Wintry Showers

Dull, snow-stained cloud over the hills showed the winter storm approaching, rapidly, from the east.

When it hit the village, driven by a gale that tore at the heavy boughs of the beech trees, the air temperature was hovering close to zero. What fell wasn't the mist of soft, slow flakes from remembered childhood but a hammering array of dry, hard fragments of ice that bit and stung before the relentless wind.

Rattling on to the path, it scrunched underfoot where it settled, while the breeze swirled crisp dry leaves into tight vortices before scattering them again. With the arrival of the strong wind, the sense of cold was intense, numbing my forehead where hair no longer protects it.

Thin bands of ice fragments started to accumulate across the meadow, marking the clumps of rush and the irregularities of the turf. The ground was solid and unyielding in the deeply crusted frost, yet still bore not-quite-random marks of exploration where the evening flock of starlings had probed the soil for food some days before.

Only later, as I climbed towards the top of the hill, did the hail slacken; the temperature seemed to rise very slightly too. The remaining particles of ice were smaller, lighter and drifted rather than fell. A single speck, no larger than an apple pip, settled on my sleeve, showing against the dark fabric as a tiny, perfect hexagon. Archetypal, embedded in our winter culture, yet something I have rarely seen.

I paused at the stile by the old quarry, resting my hand very briefly on the robust, hammered lead cap that protects the top of the gatepost.

Beyond, a group of sheep clung close to the hedgerow as they urgently grazed on the dry, yellowed grass of late winter.

As I climbed further, the cloud thinned to the east, revealing the snowfields across the uplands. The snow beyond Pendam has been on the ground for a solid month now and, as I headed back down the hill in the fading light, the wind that had been at my back now met me head-on with a thick sleet embedded in it. To describe the scene as bleak wouldn't do it justice.

Right: Afternoon sunshine contrasts with distant snow.

49. Not Quite Spring

In the last stages of its journey to the sea, the River Ystwyth curves in gentle meanders across a broad valley pasture grazed by a modest scattering of sheep.

This close to the coast, the wind from the sea is a powerful force, carving the small riverside trees into forms that leave no doubt as to its direction and persistence.

Given added impetus by the falling tide, the water moved quickly over a pebbled bed with alternating stretches of pool and riffle. Along the margin of the river, the low, matted vegetation had a pale, end-of-winter drabness despite the late-morning sunshine.

At several points, narrow gulleys led down to fans of fine sediment, which I checked, without

Left: The Afon Ystwyth as it nears the sea.
Right: The sun shines from behind a bank of cloud.

success, for the paw and tail prints of any otter that might be passing through. Close by, the flowering gorse added isolated patches of bright colour – almost matching the yellow of the blackbird's bill as it settled on the wire fence. From the depths of dormant bramble thickets, tangled and moribund, robins called and chased defiantly as they reinforced their territories.

Beyond the river, the great mass of Pen Dinas reaches steeply up from the meadows. Now topped by a monument to the Duke of Wellington, it once hosted an Iron Age fort with an enviable location. Dominating river valleys to north and south, and with ready access to good soil and the resources of both the sea and fresh water, this must have been a settlement of huge power and influence.

A pair of paragliders lifted from a field high on the seaward side and began to beat across the hillside in a manner not unlike that of the local red kites, who ignored the intrusion, calling to each other from the woodland opposite.

As I walked eastwards, a sharp-edged bank of cloud began to move inland, cutting across the sun and leaving it a chill, milky ghost; but as I crossed the river at Pont Tanycastell, a single dot of yellow on the roadside verge announced the first lesser celandine I've seen this year. A hint that spring may finally be on its way.

....

Left: A pair of paragliders above Pen Dinas.

50. Hills, a River and an Abbey

Frost still outlined the old oak leaves that lay against the dry stone wall. The sun had yet to reach the path below the hill, and despite the hints of spring in the hedgerow it felt unreasonably cold. Beyond the wall, breached here and there by the slow heave of ancient trees, the pasture sloped down toward the flood plain of the Afon Mawddach.

Once a main route, the stone bridge at Llanelltyd now carries only a quiet footpath, allowing a glimpse of a time when travel was slower paced. While not the first crossing on this site, its five elegant arches have survived the depredations of floods and traffic since the mid-18th century. I stood above one of the mid-stream cutwaters that help steer the river flow and watched the water sweep around the shoals below the bridge, then turned eastwards to see if I could catch a glimpse of the abbey through the trees.

For the Cistercian monks who founded it, the site for Cymer Abbey – located near fresh water, fishing and good pasture – must have seemed an obvious choice. Established in 1198, it never gained the wealth and degree of patronage achieved by some other abbeys, perhaps appropriately for an order based on asceticism, and well before the dissolution it was already in decline.

On this bright morning I was the only visitor to the ruins of the abbey and, walking carefully around the clumps of snowdrops in the turf, I explored the remaining walls while robins sang piercingly from the beech hedges.

Characteristic arches and some sandstone carvings survive from the small, simple buildings, and I sat in the sunshine within the walls pondering – not for the first time – whether I would have survived the rigours of medieval monastic life.

To the south, the ridges of the Cadair Idris range hung behind the trees, patches of snow still visible on the upper slopes. As I walked back towards the bridge, the profiles of the summit, a lower ridge and the nearby woodland canopy aligned to form a repeating pattern. The illusion of sweeping waves was profound, yet only visible from one corner of the path, and I wondered how many monks had paused there to remark upon it.

Left: The old bridge over the Afon Mawddach.
Right: Snow remains on the mountain tops.

Acknowledgements

There are many people to thank for helping me get this book written:

My wife and sons, who have supported me in innumerable ways and have been my companions on many of these explorations. The book is dedicated to them.

The editors I have worked with at *The Guardian*, especially Celia Locks, Anne-Marie Conway and Paul Fleckney.

My fellow writers, for their companionship and encouragement.

Those folk I have met and chatted with on my walks and who have shared their observations.

And my parents, who taught me the value of a good walk – whatever the weather.